M000077060

RE**S**TAGED

A MENTAL MODEL
FOR PERSONAL AND
PROFESSIONAL GROWTH

RESTAGED

CONROD S. J. KELLY

Author of STAGED! A Four-Step Process to Stand Out in
Your Personal and Professional Life

Copyright © 2019 by Conrod S. J. Kelly

All rights reserved. No part of this book may be reproduced
in any way including written, electronic, recording, or
photocopying without written permission of the publisher or
author. The exception would be in the case of brief
quotations embodied on the pages where the publisher or
author specifically grants permission.

Mynd Matters Publishing
715 Peachtree Street NE
Suites 100 & 200
Atlanta, GA 30308
www.myndmatterspublishing.com

ISBN: 978-0-9910859-2-7
e-ISBN: 978-0-9910859-3-4

FIRST EDITION

To Joy and Nola Grace
I am - because you are.
You are the love of my life.
You are my reason.
You are my joy.
You are my everything.

FOREWORD

A few years back, Conrod and I had the opportunity to spend time together calling on several important customers across the state of Michigan. While these calls were very productive, I found that our shared windshield time was even more rewarding and beneficial. It was during this time that I got to know Conrod better; not only on a professional level, but also a personal one – laughing at our similarities and learning from our differences.

Throughout the course of our conversations, I was eager to learn more about Conrod's journey; steps he had taken to grow and develop, people who helped mentor him, and challenges he faced and how he overcame them. It was clear to me that Conrod was invested in continuous learning and the value it offered in strengthening and developing his personal brand.

Stumbling across a webinar where Conrod served as a panel member, I listened intently to insights he provided around the topic of personal branding. He shared, "If you don't develop a brand, one will be established for you!" Boy, did that resonate with me! It was during this webinar that I also learned that Conrod had written a book entitled *STAGED*!

Of course, I purchased this book and began voraciously reading, underlining, and writing in the margins – reminders for me as I began my own developmental journey. The simple concepts outlined in *STAGED!* were easy to apply and the correlations between how one readies his house for sale and readying oneself for a new career adventure made perfect sense. One of the "asks" that Conrod set out early in this book was to teach others what you learned or discovered from reading this book. While I probably didn't recall that initially, I found myself wanting to share what I learned, not only from the webinar, but also from *STAGED!*; encouraging my colleagues to pick up the book so we could set aside time to discuss what resonated most. I joked with Conrod that I was the best publicist he never asked for!

My copy is dog-eared, over-highlighted, and continues to serve as a reference for when I'm feeling my curb appeal is not what it could be or that my brand needs de-cluttering. I highly recommend *STAGED!* to help anyone who wants to stop, start, reflect, adjust, or build on what's likely an already strong foundation. I'm blessed to call Conrod my friend and mentor. His words continue to inspire me to stretch to be my personal best!

Peggy Lemko
March 2019

CONTENTS

HABIT

I am your constant companion.

I am your greatest helper or heaviest burden.

I will push you onward or drag you down to failure. I am completely at your command.

Half of the things you do, you might as well turn over to me and I will do them—quickly and correctly.

I am easily managed—you must be firm with me. Show me exactly how you want something done and after a few lessons, I will do it automatically.

I am the servant of great people, and alas, of all failures as well. Those who are great, I have made great. Those who are failures, I have made failures. I am not a machine though I work with the precision of a machine plus the intelligence of a person.

You may run me for profit or run me for ruin—it makes no difference to me.

Take me, train me, be firm with me, and I will place the world at your feet.

Be easy with me and I will destroy you.

Who am I?

I am Habit.

—Unknown

INTRODUCTION
FEEDBACK IS TRULY A GIFT

The email below is what prompted me to write
RESTAGED. I am so grateful for this feedback.

Thursday, July 7, 2016 5:01 PM
Subject: Staged!
From: Elise

> *Hi Conrod,*
>
> *Please excuse the delay. I wanted to take time to reflect
> on my original thoughts and notes before presenting.*
>
> *As a whole, I found Staged! incredibly inspiring,
> reflection-invoking, and cool! I can't tell you how
> many passages I found myself underlining, starring
> and hearting to come back to!! I wish I had the guts
> and dedication to accomplish a book! Your willingness
> to share, solicit feedback and expose yourself to
> vulnerability is beautiful and a testament of your
> strength and confidence.*
>
> *Thank you.*
>
> *Below I've listed my feedback. Please take it with a
> grain of salt and let me know if you have any questions
> or retorts.*

Considerations:

How do the 4 steps connect to the structure/layout of the book? I found myself a little confused by the 8 chapters and how they connected back to the 4 steps.

I would have liked the completion of each step to be a "bigger deal," so that I felt encouraged and that progress was being made. I loved page 71—a big and bold announcement of my completion/success and would have liked to see that at the end of each step.

As I was reading, I found myself wanting more details about the writer and how they personally experienced, overcame, succeeded, and failed. If I am going to take advise and connect with written words, I need established credibility and trust with the author. I want to know that you put your money where your mouth is and that you did all of these things that you're telling me to do and what happened when you did them.

For instance, give an example of a time you solicited feedback. Specifically, what did you say and how did they respond? What choices did you make to accomplish your goals/dreams? Who or what have you dismissed from your life to achieve success? On Page 69, you start to give a real-life account (telling the VP you wanted to be a part of her legacy), but never finished the story. I wanted to know how she responded!!! I felt like I was left hanging.

I loved how you provided your story in the end but feel it would have been even more impactful to inject additional, relevant, personal experiences throughout the book. The Real World, Real Things moments are a great time to inject personal stories and self-reflection. I didn't always feel that the information within them directly related or connected to the subject matter and they sometimes came off as tangents.

On page 24, there's an exercise requiring you to refer back to a dream selected earlier in the book. What dream are you referencing? The only previous dream discussion was on page 16, and at the time it was my understanding that we were talking sleep dreams, not aspirations. I may have just missed it, but a reference page number would solve this!

In section 8, you gave an unbelievable account of your life and all the supporters therein. While I found it incredibly remarkable, there were times when I felt a little jealous that I hadn't been given those same opportunities or had that same level of support. Knowing you and understanding that you worked your butt off to gain those opportunities and to shine when faced with them made it easier to swallow, but for the average stranger I think it would be beneficial to include some struggles and genuine accounts of your crazy preparedness. Otherwise, the reader may feel that they can never reach your level because they'll never be presented with those same opportunities and/or never had that level of support growing up.

Loves:

I love the forced interaction and constant accountability of the reader. Physically making me take pen to paper and discuss lessons/goals w/ an outside source was GREAT! Once I started writing, I was committed!! I was no longer reading a book. I was taking steps towards self-betterment, and it felt good!

I love how real and blunt your words were. "Do not make the mistake of being all shine and no substance," really resonated with me. When I started at [my employer], everyone made assumptions about my lack of intelligence/capabilities/etc. Then, when they heard me speak or saw me present, they were shocked. I can't tell you how many times I've heard "Wow. You're not just a pretty face." But the truth is—had I not prepared for those moments, had I not worked my behind off behind the scenes, I would not have shone. That's where "Luck is what happens when preparation meets opportunity," comes into play. I love, love, LOVE this. I hate when people attribute success to luck. My presentations don't rock because I continuously have good days. They rock because I prepare, I practice, I perform, and I am always ready. Instilling that mentality is AWESOME!!!

You really force the reader to face hindrances head on, and you're not afraid to say that progression may even require professional help. It's such a relief to hear, because there's such a stigma surrounding counseling and in reality, it's a wonderful tool!

The analogy was awesome. You made me think about fixing my life without actually saying, "This is how you fix your life." The parallels were incredible, and I learned two totally different things at the same time!!

Again, thank you so much for sharing. It was a real pleasure, and I hope at least some of this is insightful.

Happy Thursday!!!

E

CHAPTER 1

TO MASTER IT, TEACH IT

As far back as I can remember, I have always enjoyed learning. It wasn't the act of acquiring knowledge I was drawn to, but the experience of achieving a deep enough level of understanding of a subject matter that I could put it into practice or, even better, teach someone else. Whether intentional or unintentional, I often found myself in "teacher" roles as I grew up, serving as a peer mediator in middle school and a tutor in high school.

One of my most memorable experiences occurred during my time at Florida A&M University's School of Business and Industry (SBI). In my business school, after the first year, every student become a teacher and remained one until graduation. Our professional development classes were two credit hours every semester but seemed to take up most of our course load. We had student-run "companies" that taught business writing, oratory skills, and business etiquette for different settings and cultures, among a host of other important topics. Even though they were managed by students, they operated like well-oiled Fortune 500 companies. Dr. Sybil Mobley, the Dean of SBI, believed the best way to produce future leaders was to consistently put them in environments that demonstrated their knowledge and skills and had them teach it to others until they achieved what she called, "unconscious competence." Unconscious competence usually happens once one has had so much practice that the skill becomes second nature.

After my matriculation, I continue to use this approach to deepen my understanding of various subjects by oscillating between student and teacher and surrounding myself with others who are committed to continuous learning. It is a habit I have developed.

In the spirit of "to master it, teach it," I have intentionally structured this book to have you take on the role of student and teacher so you too can start to develop this habit. Establishing a habit of a growth mindset is oriented around a sequence I call the Five P's: Purpose, Process, Preparation, Practice, Persistence.

1. After reading each chapter, take a couple of days to reflect on what you read. The benefits of self-reflection are endless. However, we rarely give ourselves quiet time to look within. Reflection enables you to think deeper about an issue in a relaxed state, which may potentially lead you to greater insights. An insight should help you understand the cause and effect within a specific context, such as the relationship between what you say and what you do or the implications of past and future actions. Be sure to write down the insight when it hits you.

2. Make a commitment to act on the insight by identifying one thing you will do differently and then ask someone to hold you accountable. We live in a world where we believe we can do

multiple things at once. But, there is an overwhelming body of evidence that supports doing things in sequence rather than parallel will get you more results in a shorter period of time. For example, if I give you three tasks that take three days each to complete, by doing the tasks in sequence you will finish the first in three days, the second in six days, and the last in nine days. If you do one-third of each job on each day, it will take nine days to deliver all three where you would have delivered two tasks already by day six with a sequential approach. Accountability is crucial for the work we are about to do. You will need to identify one or more individuals you trust to be honest with you and, more importantly, with whom you can be completely vulnerable. Having an accountability partner promotes commitment and gives you the confidence you need to improve. They can also help you celebrate the small wins along the way.

3. Start sharing what you're learning with people in your circle and listen carefully to how they summarize in their own words. This is a great way for you to gauge your depth of understanding. If you are like me, you may have convinced yourself you are a quick study of new concepts or ideas before.. I've learned the hard way that there is a big difference between being aware and understanding, especially when you have to apply what you think you know or explain it to

someone else. Learning something new means being clumsy at it, making mistakes, course-correcting, and trying again. It's uncomfortable and even when we know the skill is valuable, it can make our work more difficult, causing many to stop trying and revert to old habits. Having someone you can practice teaching it to and having them say it back to you will help you more accurately assess where you are on your journey to unconscious competence.

PRACTICE

If you want to develop good habits, you must embrace the act of practice. You have to be purposeful and persistent. Nothing has or can be achieved without practice. The more you practice, the more things will come to you naturally, and the more they become part of your character. As I mentioned before, it's important to share your insights, actions, and observations with others. Throughout this book, I have infused Real World, Real Things moments: personal stories and reflections to bring each concept to life.

My first Real World, Real Things moment is the origin of the phrase. My best friend Darrell and I met July 9, 2001. He was two months into his first INROADS internship with Johnson & Johnson (J&J) in their Information Technology department. Earlier that summer, three days before I was supposed to start my internship in marketing at Lucent Technologies, I learned they were scrapping the program. In 1999, as the Internet boom was approaching its apex, Lucent Technologies was the world's largest telecommunications equipment company. In high school, I'd won our class stock market challenge because of my investment in that company. However, the Internet crash in 2001 changed everything. I was beyond disappointed. The star student that landed a coveted internship was now sitting at home while his friends were at work.

After a few weeks of sulking, my mom told me to humble myself and get a regular job. What most teenagers had seen as a rite of passage (most of my friends in high school had mall jobs for pocket change or to help out at home), I saw as failure. My mother quickly helped me realize my perception was being framed by my ego.

One morning, she asked me to dress up a little and go with her somewhere. She took me to Precision Response Corporation, a call center, and made me fill out an application. I had to complete a typing test which determined if I got an interview. I passed and during the subsequent interview was asked a few straightforward questions. At the end of the interview, I was offered a job. While I waited for my background check and drug test to clear, I received a call from INROADS about the J&J internship.

Darrell and I hit it off immediately. He was my girlfriend's coffee and lunch buddy, who interned at J&J as well, and she introduced us when I started. One day over the summer, we were watching movies at his house. We started watching *The Best Man,* a classic in the African American community. Morris Chestnut, one of the main characters, was the Idris Elba of the 90s and early 2000s, sort of like a super hero for young, black males, especially those of a darker complexion. There was a scene where his character plays cards with his friends and says, "We're in the real world now…real world, real things." Then, as the camera zooms in he does a head tilt and a slight lick of his lips while the other stare at him in awe. Darrell and I looked at each other and laughed out loud to the point of tears. They sold the scene like it would go down in cinematic history. Darrell and I have since used the phrase "Real World, Real Things" anytime we hear something that should be straightforward and well understood or something that is simple but provocative.

Real World, Real Things Moment:
To Understand, You Must Overlearn

My middle school teacher Mrs. Hoffman introduced me to a type of practice that psychologists refer to as overlearning. Overlearning is practicing a skill beyond the initial achievement of mastery. I remember taking a test that I did *all right* on–I got a C—which were not all right in my home (for the record, neither were B's). It took me nearly the whole class period to finish the test and earn a C. Mrs. Hoffman knew I got picked up late from school most days, so she had me come back and retake the test but gave me less time to complete it. This time, I got a B. I was also one of the first kids to get dropped off at school, so she had me come back the next morning and take the test again with even less time. That time, I got an A. I had to keep the C I originally earned, but she demonstrated the point of investing the time upfront to practice even when I think I know the material. The fact that I was given less time and still improved my score demonstrates the mental efficiency of practice.

Because of that experience, I developed a habit of practicing and overlearning things, which made it was easier to recall what I was studying and required less time, effort, and energy.

I remember watching an interview with Michael Jordan where he was asked how he plays at such a high level in high-pressure situations. He smirked and stated it was because he had practiced those high-pressure situations since he was a kid. His preparation gave him a competitive advantage over those who hadn't because they never saw themselves playing that role.

Another example of this approach happened when I was in the fall semester of my last year in graduate school. The years of hard work had to culminate in landing a job prior to graduation. The largest career fair for MBAs is the National Black MBA Conference which averages 10,000+ attendees and over 500 companies. While I was confident in my abilities, academic preparation, and work experience, I knew I'd be going up against students from the other top MBA programs across the globe.

While on internship with J&J and GlaxoSmithKline, I volunteered to be on the diversity recruiting teams. This afforded me firsthand experience of what it was like for students and employers at big conferences. I listened carefully to all the stories about students who showed up to interviews unprepared and what that experience was like for the interviewers.

With several conferences under my belt and a catalog of insights, I went into overlearning mode. I researched books specific to the interview process for MBAs and found the one that changed my life forever–*How to Interview Like a Top MBA* by Dr. Shel Leanne. To this day, I keep five copies on hand and give them out to people who are interviewing for any role in any industry at any level.

Since I wasn't the only person with access to the book, having it didn't give me a competitive advantage. What did was being armed with the knowledge from it of what to expect at the conference. I started by reading the entire book a few times a week until I felt I'd mastered the concepts. Then, I profiled all the companies I was interested in and updated those profiles weekly leading up to the conference. I wrote down questions I would ask the CEO of each company based on the information I was gathering to use in my interviews. Finally, I practiced.

I practiced interviewing in complete silence (the early morning time slot) and at the mall (the mid-day time slots). I practiced five, ten, fifteen, thirty, forty-five, and one-hour and fifteen-minute interviews. I practiced individual and panel interviews. I practiced the conversation they didn't tell you was an actual interview. Some days, I practiced with breakfast and lunch and other days I practiced with just breakfast: a cereal bar and water. I practiced listening by going to loud establishments with friends and not missing anything in the conversation (preparation for the interview booth separated by curtains). I would even put on my dress shoes and walk around Lake Ella in Tallahassee to make sure my feet wouldn't hurt at the conference and be a distraction.

So, what happened?

I focused my efforts on eight companies and secured eight interviews prior to arriving at the conference. I interviewed from 7 AM to 6 PM and experienced all the things I prepared for, including skipping lunch. I received offers for second and third round interviews from all eight companies. By the end of the fall semester, I received eight job offers, all over six-figures in total compensation from Merck, Whirlpool, Dow Chemical, Pfizer, GlaxoSmithKline, LifeScan (J&J), Ortho Clinical Diagnostics (J&J), and Ethicon Endo Surgery (J&J). I have since worked at three of these companies and have great relationships with people at all of them.

My favorite experience was the one I knew most people hadn't prepared for. The final round of the Whirlpool interview consisted of a five-minute presentation on why you were the best candidate for the role. If you went over time, you were eliminated, and you could use any format you wanted. I had read the book *Now Discover Your Strengths* over the summer and found my five strengths were Strategic, Woo, Maximizer, Achiever, and Positivity. The first letters of these five strengths form the word SWAMP. So, I went into this presentation and told them why they should hire the "SWAMP" thing. I had so much fun because I was being 100% myself and I was confident because I had prepared.

The other candidates from Harvard, Yale, MIT, University of Michigan, and Northwestern all talked about how challenging the presentation was because they had not prepared for it. On the way back to our hotel, my phone rang but I didn't answer. When I got to my room, I listened to a voicemail from the hiring manager informing me I got the job.

CHAPTER 2

INCEPTION

Take a few minutes to reflect on the word inception as an act, process, or instance of beginning. Listed below are a few words that are synonymous with inception:

Origin, Start, Begin, Launch, Commence, Initiate

When viewing the list holistically, three themes emerge. The first two are excitement and uncertainty. While excitement tends to have a positive connotation and uncertainty leans more negative, they both draw from the same energy source—the unknown. Excitement and uncertainty can and should travel together. Throughout my life, I've used these two emotions as an indication that I'm moving in the right direction. While many of us would like to believe "knowing" would give us a sense of purpose, I've found the absence of proof to be a source of incredible strength, sometimes referred to as faith. In my experience, choosing to have faith turns uncertainty into excitement instead of fear.

Choice, the third theme, is something you will see embedded throughout the book. Nothing in this world is more powerful than choice. A life geared toward continued growth requires us to know the choices we make or don't make direct our lives.

If you are a movie aficionado, seeing *Inception* as the title of this chapter may have made you think of Christopher Nolan's 2010 blockbuster film. The movie's central theme is that an idea can be a powerful force. Without giving a full synopsis, *Inception* follows a group of individuals attempting to plant an idea in a target's mind while the target is dreaming. The "extractor" knows how to influence the individual to reveal their deepest thoughts–he is in search of insight.

Another character, "the architect," is charged with creating an environment filled with details from an individual's own subconscious and memories. By having the subject fill in all the details, it convinces him that the dream world is real.

We can all use someone that can help us look within to uncover what might be holding us back from exposing or expressing our best self. When we feel stuck, changing our environment can be one way to change our mood. This frees up more space for introspection.

Real World, Real Things Moment:
Manipulation Through Inspiration

Since my inception, no one has been more methodical at planting ideas in my head than my mother. I now realize my five-foot-two mother, with her big smile and even bigger heart, is the most manipulative person in my life, but in the best way. She always had words of inspiration like:

- Just doing the homework assigned means everyone is on the same page but going ahead gives you an advantage.
- Practice until you can do it without thinking.
- Bad practice will get you bad results. Excellent

practice will get you excellent results.

- Always be on your best behavior because you never know who is watching.

As an adult, I have come to realize the wisdom in her ways. The best example of my mother's manipulation was her calling me her little genius. By calling me a genius, she helped me develop self-esteem and confidence at an early age. Because I believed in myself, I worked my butt off to make sure my grades and accolades reflected my genius status. When I came across the quote below, it all seemed to make sense.

"Genius is one percent inspiration and ninety-nine percent perspiration." —Thomas Edison

LET YOUR DREAMS BE YOUR GUIDE

How often have you heard the phrase, "Dream Big?" A key point in that phrase is the idea that you're in the driver's seat. Your dreams are not a departure from reality. They are the catalyst taking you from your current reality to your desired truth.

One of the most famous dreams is memorialized in Dr. Martin Luther King, Jr.'s "I Have a Dream" speech. His dream was a roadmap for how we, as a nation, could evolve from a state of inequality to a place where all men are treated as equals. Many speculate that Dr. King knew he would not live to see his dream achieved. But it was his faith, the substance of things hoped for and evidence of things not seen, that allowed him to keep pushing. Within the speech he laid out several goals for the country.

Goals are mile markers to let you know if you are making progress. They remind us that the road to success is paved with small wins. When you start the staging process in later chapters, you will see each step requires you to set a goal. I am going to assume most of you have had a dream of doing something great before. However, some of you may not know where to start. Some of you may have put that dream on the back burner. Some of you may have even given up on the dream altogether. It is my intent to help you achieve that dream by giving you tools to unearth the most important ingredient to sustained personal and professional growth—your authentic self.

BRINGING IT HOME

Much like the characters in *Inception*, for the remainder of *RESTAGED*, I will play the role of your architect and extractor. You will be presented with ideas and questions that will ask you to make choices and reflect in search of insight. To do this, I have developed a process based on the principles of home staging and included worksheets for you to take notes and answer questions.

You may dismiss these principles based on their simplicity, but I hope you do not. Robin Sharma said it best with, "Simplicity is the trademark of genius."

CHAPTER 3

HOME STAGING AS A MENTAL MODEL FOR GROWTH

THE BIG STAGE

One of the fastest growing trends in real estate is home staging. Although some of you may be familiar with it, and have even used it in the past, for others, it is an unknown concept.

Model homes, malls, department stores, car showrooms, grocery stores, and hotels are laid out in a specific way to focus your attention on what, how, and when they want you to see things. Yes, they are staged! Similar to the dream world in *Inception*, it is you who projects your thoughts and emotions into these environments that drive your beliefs and behaviors.

BE INTENTIONAL

In the next four chapters, I am going to leverage the principles of home staging as a practical process for you to apply in matters of personal and professional growth and development. Although the principles may sound obvious, growth doesn't happen by chance. It is a choice to be uncomfortable with being comfortable because nothing grows in a comfort zone. Again and again, points of comfort will arise. It's your responsibility to routinely choose to grow.

Growth flourishes at the intersection of purpose, process, preparation, practice, and persistence. It comes from a commitment to overlearning good habits and unlearning bad ones. It is often the things we are unwilling to release and remove that stall our growth rather than the things we have yet to learn.

My goal is to provide you with a model that helps you make these choices. Your superpower is your ability to choose. After learning Seneca Roman's quote, "Luck is what happens when preparation meets opportunity," it made sense why those who *choose* to be prepared are very lucky.

COMPETITIVE ADVANTAGE

At its core, home staging is about gaining a competitive advantage over similar homes in the area. It comes down to determining what or who your competition is and what changes would level the playing field or, better yet, give you an edge.

While it is often easy to identify the external competitor, take into consideration that doubt, fear, anger, bad habits, complacency, and lack of preparation can also be competitors. Sometimes the choices we make, or fail to make, and the stories we tell ourselves make us our own worst enemy and erode our confidence.

What is a personal or professional goal that you would like to accomplish?

_____

_____

_____

_____

What makes you best suited to accomplish your goal from above?

_____

_____

_____

_____

Who or what is your competition?

_____

_____

_____

_____

Who or what could get in the way of you achieving your goal?

_____

_____

_____

_____

Real World, Real Things Moment:
Renting vs. Buying

I've had numerous debates with friends about whether buying or renting is the smarter financial decision. Ultimately, the conversation tends to end with, "It depends." There are definitely times where renting is a better option than owning. Renting often requires less money upfront, but you don't build equity. When renting, the repairs are typically less and may be covered by the landlord, but there are restrictions on how much you can personalize the space. Over time, the monthly rental fee normally increases, whereas in owning a home the value typically increases. Renting gives you the flexibility to move whenever you like, while home ownership normally requires more commitment. The longer you stay in a home, the more equity and personal wealth you are able to build.

My theory is that a lot of people in this world rent their goals rather than own them. Many of us grew up with rented goals from our parents, teachers, or mentors. Those rented goals were great in small doses as inspiration and direction. However, think about the last time you rented a car or stayed in a hotel room. Did you wash, wax, or vacuum your rental car? Did you make up the bed and clean the bathroom in your hotel room? When you rent things, you depend on the person who owns it to do the maintenance. When you own it, it is up to you, even if you have to pay someone to help you. Although on occasion, I have encountered people living in a home they own with a renter's mindset.

It is beneficial to inherit goals that give us direction and purpose, but there will come a time when you have to decide if those rented goals are right for you. Unlike the many scenarios you have to consider when deciding to rent or own a home, the decision to own your goals should be more straightforward.

LOVE IT OR LIST IT

The staging process and model will present you with an opportunity to reshape how you see yourself and how others see you. After taking the steps to stage a home, many people often change their mind about selling because they find new reasons to love it again.

<u>Real World, Real Things Moment:</u>
We Love It

My wife and I are huge fans of HGTV. One of our favorite shows is *Love It or List It* where interior designer Hilary Farr and real estate agent David Visentin compete for the affections of fed-up homeowners looking to either renovate or sell. Farr transforms their worn-out space while Visentin finds them a new home. At the end of each hour-long episode, the homeowners decide if the changes designed by Farr are enough for them to stay in their current home, or if the new property Visentin has found better suits their needs. Whether they love it or list it, the homeowners come out on top. The same is true for the process in *RESTAGED*. If you choose to make improvements to support a goal and end up staying the course, you are still in a better position after having done the work.

ADD VANTAGE

Home staging involves accentuating the home's advantages and eliminating or reducing perceived negatives. Staging focuses on using presentation to shape how buyers perceive your home and its features. When staging a home, the intent should not be to focus on your own taste or comfort zone, but on the buyers who will be attracted to your house.

What have you done to accentuate your advantages and eliminate or reduce your perceived weaknesses?

_____

_____

_____

_____

CHANGE CREATES CHANGE ($)

Taking the time to stage a home can pay off big. Complete renovations are rare, but there will certainly be some essential changes needed. By choosing to stage a home, it's possible to have a quicker sale and larger return. Many real estate agents will only list a home if it has been staged. They know how much easier and more profitable the transaction will be if the investment—of time, effort, and money—has been made. By staging, all the work for potential buyers has already been done. They do not have to imagine the home's potential. The necessary preparations were already taken to show the home at its best.

A STAGING MINDSET

So far, I have presented the concept of home staging as a process to undertake when selling a home. While you could stage yourself to achieve a short-term goal, staging should be a mental model for sustained personal and professional growth.

A mental model is an explanation of how things work. It guides our perceptions and behaviors. They are the thinking tools used to understand life, make decisions, and solve problems. If you choose to make the staging approach your new way of thinking and behaving, you will develop habits that create life-altering results.

As stated earlier, it is the choices we make or fail to make that change our circumstances. Seemingly small changes can make a tremendous difference. However, just because something may seem small does not mean it only requires a small amount of effort. Growth requires continuous effort. Even small amounts of effort sustained over a period of time can lead to great results. The motto for my business school really captured it best— *"No excuse is acceptable. No amount of effort is adequate until proven effective."* Do not fall victim to working overtime to avoid putting in the effort needed for your goal.

Real World, Real Things Moment:
Are You Running in the Right Direction?

A few months ago, I struggled with a professional challenge and I connected with several mentors for advice on how best to manage it. As I reflected on their guidance, I realized there was a central theme in the questions they posed to me:

Are you running in the right direction?

I consider myself a good problem solver, thanks to my schooling. I was exposed to programs like Odyssey of the Mind, Future Business Leaders of America, and a rigorous curriculum at Florida A&M University's School of Business and Industry. My upbringing also had a lot to do with it. The situations that made me feel unlucky taught me invaluable problem-solving skills. At one point, I thought problems kept finding me. But, my perspective changed when I received the best career advice I could ask for—run towards problems. Turns out, that is what I had been doing my whole life.

If the only constant in the world is change, there will always be problems to solve. There is nothing people fear more than change. Those who fear change turn their backs on success. creating opportunities for those who see change as an opportunity to make progress.

To achieve personal or professional success, you need a bit of luck. As mentioned earlier, luck is something you create because it is the intersection of preparation and opportunity. If you believe that there is a relationship between change and problems, then running towards problems will always create more opportunities. But those opportunities will only be available to you if you have prepared. When you are trying to tackle a hard problem, you have to be at your best. Fortunately, or unfortunately, that is when everyone is watching.

I walked away from my discussions with three pieces of advice. First, I had to gain perspective on what was working and not just what wasn't. What was working should help me overcome the situation. Secondly, I had to run towards the problem, not away from it. By leaning in, I was able to see the issue more clearly. Running from it put my back toward the issue. Lastly, I made time to listen to others. The feedback I was getting helped me change the conversation I was having with myself and be more positive. What really drove the advice home were two statements. First, there is no better personal brand than being a **problem solver.** Second, the organization puts their best and brightest on the biggest problems and the areas with the most opportunity. Some may say those people are just lucky, but now you know why.

RETURN ON INVESTMENT

According to the National Association of Realtors Home Staging Statistics in 2017:

- Staged homes sell 88% faster and for 20% more than non-staged ones.
- 38% of sellers' agents said they stage all homes prior to listing them for sale.
- The most common home improvement practices agents recommended to sellers were decluttering the home (93%) and entire home cleaning (89%).

A survey by Homegain.com reported that people who spent $500 on staging recovered over 343% of the cost when they sold their home. Imagine the returns you could have just by investing in yourself. If you use the proper sequence, staging can help you make exponential gains towards your goals.

By taking you through each step of the staging process, it is my intention to help you become more self-aware. Self-awareness is an exercise in discovering, accepting, and acting upon the truth. When you are self-aware, you can be honest about who you are and what you want to be. If you decide to go through this process, you will be presented with a choice to act on the insights you unearth along the way. If you choose not to, then you are the owner of the outcomes associated with not acting. You must be willing to do the work to achieve your desired results.

There are four key principles in home staging:
1. Insight: Do Your Homework
2. Invest: Declutter, Clean, and Repair
3. Interest: Illuminate Your Curb Appeal
4. Inspire: Tell Your Story

A few last words of encouragement before you start...

May your choices reflect your hopes, not your fears.
—Nelson Mandela

Sometimes the wrong choices bring us to the right places.
Sometimes you make choices in life and sometimes choices
make you.
Freedom is realizing you have a choice.
—T. F. Hodge

CHAPTER 4

INSIGHT

OH SNAP!

The first step in home-staging requires looking at a home through the eyes of a potential buyer. One of the best ways to view a home in a new light is through photography. It has a unique ability to capture what the eye does not see. Photos reveal exactly how a home looks to outsiders, which aids in identifying the necessary changes that need to be made. One cannot fix a problem he does not know exists.

ROSES

There is an old saying that an arrogant person walks around like their "shit" doesn't smell. OutKast, the former Atlanta-based rap duo, used this saying in their hit song *Roses*. Passing the sniff test is a huge part of home staging. You not only have to consider what a potential buyer sees, but also what he or she may smell. Those that know their home has a bad smell in specific rooms or throughout the house often make the mistake of trying to cover up the smells rather than fixing it from the source. No matter how large or exquisite a home is, if it has a bad smell, it will be much harder to sell. Every home has a scent, but unless the owner gets feedback from someone who doesn't live in it, they'll never know if it's a deterrent to someone buying it.

Real World, Real Things Moment:
The difference makes a difference

A few years ago, I lead a team that had a tremendous amount of success. The performance helped me earn a promotion to lead a bigger team in a different part of the organization. I was very excited because I had great momentum. I had figured out how to launch a product successfully, build a highly functional team, and create a culture of excellence. I jumped into my new role and started setting up meetings, making decisions, and trying to implement my old playbook with my new team. I'll cut to the chase and let you know that it initially didn't go well. With the help of my HR business partner, we solicited feedback from the team and narrowed the issue down to one fact: I didn't check in to get their input with what was working, what wasn't working, what they felt we needed to do, and most importantly, their biggest concerns in having a new leader come in. We ended up having a very insightful conversation, which began a tremendous transformation to the culture of the team and our ability to deliver innovation to our customers. This helped me become more self-aware that the "scent" from my previous role wasn't as appealing to them—so we worked together on a new fragrance.

THE SNIFF TEST

While having good hygiene and a home that doesn't smell is important, the sniff test is actually a metaphor for feedback. When you get so close or attached to who you are or who you think you are - your ego - it is often difficult to see your blind spots. The best antidote to ego is feedback. Feedback gives you knowledge.

The more you know, the more you realize what you don't know, which keeps the ego in check. Most of us have aspects and traits that are obvious to everyone but ourselves, so be intentional about asking a diverse set of people to give you a sniff.

"I See," said the Blind Man.

The range of what we think and do is limited by what we fail to notice. And because we fail to notice that we fail to notice, there is little we can do to change: until we notice how failing to notice shapes our thoughts and deeds.
—R.D. Laing

Blinds spots can be hard to find because they are often buried in denial. The sometimes unpleasant nature of the truth and perception that feedback is accusatory creates an inability to recognize or unwillingness to deal with the proverbial elephant in the room. Denial is a close relative of fear, which functions to protect the ego and requires a substantial investment of energy. Redirecting that energy to search for your blind spots can be difficult, but it can lead to significant insights. Identifying your own blind spots is an exercise in contradiction. If you can see them, they are no longer blind to you. So how do you find your blind spots? Blind spots are repetitive experiences that make you question why something always happens to you. For example: you keep ending up in jobs you hate, you always have a terrible boss, you always have "bad luck," or people consistently perceive you differently than you see yourself. If the evidence suggests you have blind spots, you can try to eliminate them by asking yourself, "Why am I afraid to see what is really happening?" Fear is the archenemy of acceptance.

While tackling your fears can lead to some meaningful insights, the better approach may be soliciting feedback from others. I recommend starting with someone close to you and then branching out. Astonishingly, relative strangers are often the best resources for feedback. Even though I know how valuable honest feedback can be, I still have to force myself to ask for it. Any form of feedback is scary, but the kind that tackles your blind spots can be unbearable. That's why, before you ask for honest feedback, you should have a strategy in place.

The best tool you have for handling solicited feedback is choice. You can choose the date, time, location, length, topics, and objectives. For the feedback session to be meaningful, be in a place where you are open to receiving it. Here are some other tips you can use while receiving feedback.

- Consider the source and their intent.
- Listen actively to *what* is said and *how* it is said.
- Summarize what you hear to confirm you are interpreting it correctly.
- Ask clarifying questions.
- Focus on the facts and not opinions.
- Identify one or two things you agree with that you can act on and put a plan in place.

Real World, Real Things Moment:

The Coincidence of Silent and Listen

I was listening to the news one morning while getting dressed for work and I heard someone say, "You know, silent and listen are basically the same word." I didn't think much about it at first, but as I was finishing my breakfast, I realized that silent and listen are anagrams. Of the common anagrams, these two have an interesting relationship.

On my commute to work, I got a phone call from a close friend who needed to vent and asked if I had a few minutes to listen. Coincidence? This particular friend usually called for advice, but given the events of the morning, I agreed and sat quietly on the line. I learned that morning how important it sometimes is to just listen.

In today's society, advice is abundant but there seems to be a shortage of people actually listening. While feedback is a powerful gift, giving someone your undivided attention can be just as powerful, if not more.

"One of the sincerest forms of respect is actually listening to what another has to say." —Bryant H. McGill

I've heard people say they are working to improve their communication skills. However, it is rare to find anyone actively working on improving his or her listening skills. Conversation is the cornerstone of building personal and professional relationships. The foundation of a good conversation is listening. Listening builds trust and respect, enables information sharing, and encourages collaborative problem solving. People need to know their opinions matter and that you are listening without judgment. One of the best things you can do every day is give someone the simple gift of listening.

> *"Most people do not listen with the intent to understand;*
> *they listen with the intent to reply."*
> —Stephen R. Covey

My approach to becoming a better listener is to prepare for the conversation, limit the amount of time I spend speaking, and remove potential distractions. During the conversation, I try to be mindful of each of our body languages and occasionally paraphrase what I'm hearing. At the end of the conversation, I always say thank you. It seems obvious, but it doesn't happen as often as you think.

> *"Most of the successful people I've known are the ones who*
> *do more listening than talking."* —Bernard Baruch

APPRAISAL

The homework process in home staging requires finding out the features, conditions, and asking prices of competing homes. Knowing this determines how much time and money to invest in staging a home and identifies where the competition has an advantage or is vulnerable. In real estate, this is sometimes referred to as an appraisal. One of the best resources for getting this information is a real estate agent or an appraiser.

LEARN TO LEAD

To remain current and competitive, you must be a continuous learner. Just like homes have market values, so do people. Your market value increases as you gain knowledge, which helps you make better decisions. While you can try tackling the process on your own, seeking the help and wisdom of others can be invaluable.

Anyone who has had success has had the assistance, guidance, feedback, or support of someone else. You can learn a great deal from your own personal failures, but you can learn even more from the failures of others. The best way to become a continuous learner is to not fear feedback or making choices. When we choose, good or bad, we learn.

STEPPING UP

Congratulations! You have just finished learning the first step in the staging process. You've taken a big step in just a few pages. While I know you may be tempted to turn to the next chapter, I'd like for you to honor the process by taking time to reflect. It is often in times of stillness and silence that "aha" moments rise to the surface.

When I started this journey back in 2006, my insight was that if not checked, my ego would be my downfall. I came to this insight through self-reflection, feedback from friends, and time spent with a professional counselor. I had always seen my ego as a necessary evil to bolster my self-esteem, but it began to threaten my personal and professional relationships long after my self-esteem was fixed. Then, what seemed like divine intervention, I had two friends tell me about two different books they were reading.

The first was *One Day My Soul Just Opened Up* by Iyanla Vanzant. The other was *A New Earth* by Eckhart Tolle. While one book distanced me from the ego, the other helped me find and embrace my authentic self. In *A New Earth*, Tolle describes how our attachment to the ego creates the dysfunction that leads to anger, jealousy, and unhappiness. It shows readers how to awaken to a new state of consciousness and follow the path to a fulfilling existence.

One Day My Soul Just Opened Up is a 40-day program of inspiration and motivation that helps you work through problems to improve your emotional and spiritual health. Through exercises and readings, Iyanla Vanzant provides tools to tap into your strengths and open your mind, heart, and soul to the truth of your identity as a creative and powerful being.

The ego is always lurking; it is a battle I fight often to keep it at bay. In one of my last in-depth conversations with a friend that I ultimately lost to cancer, she told me to be humble and God would handle the rest. B HUMBL is now on my license plate so that I am reminded daily of her instructions and can spread her message to others.

Things to remember:
- Feedback is a gift.
- Ask for help in identifying your blind spots. You cannot fix a problem you do not know exists.

- Denial, a close relative of fear, works to protect the ego.
- Be a continuous learner by not avoiding making choices.

After reading this chapter and taking some time to reflect, I am now aware of:

_____

_____

_____

_____

The key ideas I wish to remember and share are:

_____

_____

_____

_____

I am going to apply what I have discovered by:

_____

_____

_____

_____

I am going to ask the following individual(s) to hold me accountable:

_____

_____

_____

_____

I will share my progress with them on (insert date):

_____/ _____/ _____

CHAPTER 5

INVEST

God, grant me the serenity to accept the things I cannot change; courage to change the things I can; and wisdom to know the difference. —Reinhold Niebuhr

SIGNIFICANCE OF SEQUENCE (SOS)

Declutter. Clean. Repair. I have learned there is tremendous significance in sequencing. You must crawl before you walk and walk before you run. Whether the job of an airline pilot or doctor in an emergency room, checklists are used to make sure you follow the proper sequence to improve safety and reduce errors. Sequence should have the same level of importance in your personal and professional life. When it comes to your career, business decisions, or relationships, you should give careful consideration to the sequence of your approach. The next step in the home staging process is to invest time to declutter.

COLLECTIBLES

In home staging, one of the biggest distractions is an overly cluttered home. What one may see as a collectible, someone else may see as clutter. The attachments people have to their *stuff*, make seeing it as clutter difficult, but buyers will spot it immediately. It's quite similar to having blind spots.

Clutter eats up space, limiting the ability to grow or

expand. It is connected to chaos, which breeds confusion. Distracted buyers don't see the home or themselves in the home. All they see is the homeowner's stuff. To avoid this potentially costly error, most real estate agents encourage home owners to declutter a home before taking photos and listing it.

Decluttering is not getting rid of all evidence of who you are to create a false image. When you pursue a goal, the role of your belongings changes. They now need to support your goals. The intent is to eliminate anything that may be distracting or offensive to someone who can help you accomplish your goal. Getting rid of things from the past makes room for the present and the future. It is important for you to always save room for opportunity. It does not run on a set schedule. If opportunity is not predictable, what can be? You! You can be prepared for that moment when opportunity does knock. Decluttering is your chance to remove physical and emotional attachments so that you can get to the next phase of the process: cleaning.

What clutter (people, things, emotional attachments, etc.) needs to be removed from your life in order for you to accomplish your personal or professional goals?

_____

_____

_____

_____

Real World, Real Things Moments:
Hoarding

Some of you may be fans of the TV show *Hoarders*. If you have seen the show, I'm sure during at least one episode, if not all of them, you had to look away from the TV. While the shocking images revealed the dark side of extreme compulsive hoarding, the comments from the cleanup specialist and psychologist highlight that we all do a little hoarding in our own way. We hold on to negative things people have done or said to us, previous failures or disappointments, and unsubstantiated ideas about ourselves. Many people with compulsive hoarding do not recognize the extent of the issue. Often, a family member is bothered or concerned by the clutter and brings it to their attention. Similar to blind spots and denial, we've become so used to living with certain thoughts and experiences that we do not see the impact they have on us and those around us.

Elise asked me a very direct question in her feedback about what or who I had removed from my life to achieve success. As a young, black male, six-feet four-inches tall and over 200 pounds since fourteen, my presence has always made me standout. Having a certain level of intelligence turned standing out into being a target. In middle and high school, I had two situations where a teacher's prejudice led them to grade my work differently resulting in me missing the A honor roll. Both situations were contested and reversed. In high school, one of those teachers and my counselor contacted my mother and suggested I leave my magnet school, where I was in the gifted program and advanced placement classes, to attend Job Corps to learn a trade because my failing Advanced Placement Calculus II grade meant I wouldn't have a shot at college. I've been pulled over more times than I care to remember, even had a weapon drawn on me after calling the cops because my car had been broken into. I've witnessed a neighbor lock her door as I walked across the street because I was wearing a hooded sweatshirt of my alma mater instead of the business clothes she sees me in when I leave out in the morning. I've been followed and ignored in stores, and even received different medical care until I start asking questions that showed my understanding of medicine and the health care system. I've had colleagues and superiors try to ruin my career because I was a threat to what they felt they were entitled to.

So, who did I choose to remove? I didn't have to remove anyone. Those people represented micro-moments in the span of a lifetime and I know there will be others. But what they did and said had the potential to stay with me forever and eat away at my soul. So, my decluttering involved choosing love over hate. Forgiveness over anger. Being open instead of closed off. Trust over distrust. Thinking before acting. Listening more than speaking. Looking ahead instead of looking back. Choosing my truth over their lies. Choosing not to be a victim. It always comes back to choice.

While I first thought laziness caused hoarding, I now know it's a mental disorder that makes it difficult to make choices or see the impact their inability or unwillingness to choose has on themselves and those around them.

Hoarders taught me that there is a significant difference between making a sacrifice and making a choice. When you feel like you are forced to choose between a restricted set of options, the ego plants ideas that lead to anger, defeat, and resentment. It turns you into a victim. But when you choose to view it as a choice, you tap into that power. Choosing puts you in control and makes you accountable, which means you can change the situation by making another choice. Accountability tethers obligations to outcomes.

What choices are you prepared to make to accomplish your goals?

_____

_____

_____

_____

I hope it is clear why I introduced hoarding as we discuss decluttering. My goal was not to diagnose everyone as a hoarder. But, I strongly believe we can all remember times when we found ourselves struggling to process information, letting go of certain beliefs about our possessions, or experiencing emotional distress when asked to make a choice. Keep in mind that most hoarders require professional help. Hoarder or not, making decisions can be difficult, and sometimes you need the help of an expert.

MR. CLEAN

Decluttering allows you to see what needs to be cleaned. By removing unnecessary items, there is less *stuff* to clean, meaning cleaning will take less effort and time. A clean house shows pride of ownership, increases comfort, eliminates odors, and makes a home feel more spacious.

<u>Real World, Real Things Moments:</u>
Back, Front, Up, Down

My mother always instructed me to clean from top to bottom and back to front. I did it because she told me to, but as I started writing this chapter, her instruction took on new meaning. When you start at the bottom, you run the risk of the stuff at the top falling back down and prolonging the process. Cleaning from the back of the house helps you to not backtrack dirt into rooms that have already been cleaned.

CLEAN SLATE

"Start by doing what's necessary; then do what's possible; and suddenly you are doing the impossible."
—St. Francis of Assisi

So, what does all of this mean? Sequence is a critical component of efficiently achieving your goals. While you may be willing to let go of certain things, you also have to be willing to clean up what's left in a way that doesn't allow the dirt to creep back into your life.

Think back to the sniff test and blind spots. How do you make sure those issues don't resurface? Planning, practicing, and persisting will help you develop good habits. Good habits are your best defense against old, bad habits. To create an environment for new habits to flourish, introduce some new people, processes, and ideas and give others a one-way ticket out of your life.

LICENSE, PLEASE.

No matter how well a home is decluttered and cleaned, it won't sell if it needs serious repairs. Before a home can be sold, many states require a licensed home inspector's approval. A thorough inspection includes examining everything from the foundation to the roof. They look at significant defects and safety considerations. An inspection can then be used as a guide to address a home's major issues.

While the homeowner can handle some issues, others that have been festering for years or that can lead to unintended consequences should be managed by a specialist. Homeowners are often hesitant to spend money to fix a home just to sell it. I am a strong believer in the idea that you either pay now or end up paying later. Failure to make required repairs is a failure to adequately prepare, which preemptively limits the potential of the home.

Real World, Real Things Moments:
Personal Home Inspection

Everyone should have a "personal home" inspector. A mentor, counselor, coach, pastor, family member or friend are all good options. They can be extremely helpful in your quest to understand what needs to be fixed in your personal or professional life to help you accomplish your goals. Failure to make the necessary repairs means all the work you may have done to this point has been in vain.

One of the best things I've ever done for myself was speak to a licensed counselor. While I had done a lot of work on my own, I really needed her expertise to understand why I felt the way I did, why I did the things I did, and how I could take the proper steps to make sure the beliefs I discarded, behaviors I cleaned up, and relationships I repaired stayed that way. The counselor was extremely helpful in pointing out how things from my personal life were impacting my beliefs and behavior in a professional setting. Do not let failure to ask for help limit your potential and kill your buzz.

BUZZ KILL

If a listed home that still needs repairs does not sell, the buzz factor, which is difficult to regenerate, is gone. While cliché, it still holds true that you never get a second chance to make a first impression. A home can be ready for sale in a matter of weeks with proper planning, but it should not be rushed. Certain activities need to be tackled in a certain order or the whole process may grind to a halt.

Real World, Real Things Moments:
Red Light. Green Light

Some of you may remember the phrase, "Be home when the street lights come on." It was a popular phrase from a time when kids actually played outside. When it was time to go home, if we asked nicely, our parents would let us play "Red Light, Green Light" in the quad of our apartment complex. One person would be the stop light and the other children would assemble up at the starting line about fifteen feet away. The stop light would face away from the others and yell, "Green light!". At this point you moved towards them until they yelled, "Red light!" and turned around. If you were still moving when they turned around, you were out. Occasionally, they would yell, "Yellow light!". Play resumed when the stop light turned back around and said green light. The stop light won if all the kids were out before anyone was able to touch him or her. Otherwise, the first player to touch the stop light won the game and earned the right to be the next stop light.

So, what can we learn from "Red Light, Green Light"? Sometimes rushing into something doesn't give you the ability to stop before it's too late. It is okay to occasionally pause or proceed slowly—you may actually last longer than those who went out quickly. Standing still may actually give you an advantage. In "Red Light, Green Light," you have zero chance of losing if you aren't caught moving. You have to know the rules of the game and how to make them work to your advantage. You don't have to run. You could walk, crawl, or hop. You also don't have to move forward on every turn. You could move left or right to position yourself behind someone else. The same could be said for career moves, where lateral moves to gain broader experience or getting behind a leader that believes in talent development could ultimately catapult your career.

Even if you lose one round, there is always another opportunity. If the same person is still in charge, you will be able to apply what you learned from defeat to help you win. The person in charge can also change, which may give you a fresh start. Just remember, sometimes the lesson learned from defeat only applies to that individual or situation. Don't try to apply it to a situation where a problem doesn't exist or a situation you don't fully understand.

Trying to win too quickly can cost you a victory. In "Red Light, Green Light", if you are the last person left, why rush and risk being caught moving? I've been in situations where I would have missed a golden opportunity because I was impatient.

INSIDE OUT AND OUTSIDE IN

How many opportunities might you have missed because you were not prepared? I normally don't dwell on the past, but sometimes looking back provides perspective that lets you confidently move forward. Unless you continuously work on improving by taking an objective look and enlisting the support of others, you may find yourself in a pattern of missed opportunities.

When was the last time you took inventory of what is most important to you? In a world of limited resources, are you spending your time and energy and where you want to? What if giving up some of your stuff gave you more time or energy to invest in your goals or in others?

This part of the staging process is the most difficult because it deals with two issues that most people struggle with: comfort and risk.

Real World, Real Things Moments:
Grow Where You are Planted

As a people-leader at my company, I am often sought out for career advice. Most people want to discuss how they can get to their next role or the next level within the company while others are battling with whether or not they should move outside the company. Before I say anything, I like to ask a question that almost always seems to change the nature of the conversation: "Are you growing where you're planted?"

Throughout your career, it is not uncommon to question if you're on the right path or growing at the right pace. These feelings often spring up when a job doesn't feel as satisfying as expected. More often than not, the default thinking is to uproot and start over somewhere else or venture out on your own. I'll be the first to say I have left an organization, stayed at an organization, and started my own. All of these decisions had a positive impact—not necessarily a financial gain—on my career because the decision to stay, leave, or venture out was made based on asking myself the same question I pose to others.

There are a few tips I share with people on how they can grow where they're planted or determine if they are ready for the next opportunity. I start off by telling people to dig deeper. Connecting with people in their network is a good way to learn about opportunities that might align with their interests and provide a venue for them to get feedback. That feedback may also prompt them to see their role differently and identify ways to improve their performance. Their poor performance could have been why they were not happy in the role to begin with.

Another approach is to plant seeds. Sometimes the lack of career growth is from not planting enough seeds. I have spoken with far too many people who were disappointed about not being considered for certain roles, even though they hadn't communicated their interest or positioned their experiences with the hiring manager. Those seeds require cultivating.

The feeling of being stuck in a job, career, or even relationship is often caused by complacency. Complacency is a weed that can limit your ability to grow. Sometimes we need to remove some long-held beliefs (pull the weeds) to open ourselves up to new opportunities.

When all else fails, transplanting can be a great option. Seeds are often started in optimal conditions, like a greenhouse, then replanted somewhere else. Some of us may have been in locations for too long and the time has come to move so we can continue to grow. The corporate journey is no longer a ladder but more of a lattice. A step down or to the side may be the best approach to move up. Nevertheless, moving on is the best opportunity for growth. The work you do before leaving will help you grow where you are planted next.

Depending on your personality, comfort and risk can

be equally enjoyable or scary. When was the last time you took a risk? Unless you take risks, you will not be stretched. You will not grow, and you will not gain. Once you have completed your homework, decluttered, cleaned, and made the required repairs, the next step is to check out the view from the curb.

After reading this chapter and taking some time to reflect, I am now aware of:

_____

_____

_____

_____

The key ideas I wish to remember and share are:

_____

_____

_____

_____

I am going to apply what I have discovered by:

_____

_____

_____

_____

I am going to ask the following individual(s) to hold me accountable:

_____

_____

_____

_____

I will share my progress with them on (insert date):

_____/ _____/ _____

Things to remember:

- There is significance in sequence.
- When you decide to pursue a new goal, the role of your past, the people in your life, and your personal belongings must change to support your objective.
- Because opportunity is unpredictable, you must always strive to be prepared.
- Having a plan and executing it regularly are the key to building good habits.
- Some repairs require the help of a specialist.

CHAPTER 6
INVITE

WATTS UP?

Curb appeal is the overall impression the front of a home makes. Prospective buyers will formulate an opinion about the exterior of a home in the first fifteen seconds and it will set their expectations for the interior. The view from the curb often determines whether a buyer will consider giving a home a closer look. Any signs of neglect can instantly make them turn away. I always thought curb appeal was about landscaping. However, I now understand it includes your roof, doors, windows, garage doors, mailbox, and lighting. Of all these items, lighting is the superstar of curb appeal. Most staging resources emphasize high-wattage lightbulbs to make a home stand out. A lightbulb went off in my head—pun intended—that made me think about what "wattage" I would be if I were a lightbulb. How about you? Are you a forty, sixty, or hundred-watt lightbulb?

Real World, Real Things Moment:
Are You a Hidden Gem or Are You Hiding?

A hidden gem is an individual who is extremely talented but flying under the radar. As a people-leader, I'm often engaged in conversations with peers who are disappointed by the lack of talent and ironically, employees that are frustrated by the lack of opportunities for advancement. Why are these two groups not finding each other?

The answer is multi-factorial and I will not pretend to know the exact reason. I do believe the disconnect has as much to do with the individuals as it does the managers, the human resource processes and systems, and archaic organizational cultures.

What percent of your organization is made up of hidden gems hiding in plain sight? Regardless the percentage, both groups are detrimental to any organization. On one hand, there is wasted potential for not tapping into that hidden gem. On the other, there is wasted opportunity since the hider could be occupying an ideal spot for a hidden gem. The hider could also be a hidden gem, just in the wrong environment to unleash their potential.

Some of these individuals go undiscovered because of the bias of people-leaders and HR tools used to assess talent. These tools sometimes rely on past individual performances, which can be impacted by several factors and assumptions made by managers on potential. Academia has long proven that individual performance is not a predictor of a good leader in the same way high performance is not a predictor of high potential.

Since we will never live in a world without bias and no one has yet found the panacea for talent management, our greatest opportunity is to lean on leadership qualities to find those hidden gems and shine a light on those hiding in the cracks. Although I've worked for five different organizations, certain leadership qualities like integrity, collaboration, result-orientation, urgency, talent development, adaptability, and disciplined risk-taking, have been mainstays. If you want to be seen as a gem, you have to ensure these leadership qualities are on full display.

Below are a few things to try:

Make yourself easier to find by expanding your internal and external networks, increasing your visibility. It's also a good way to enlist others in getting the word out about you. There is nothing great leaders love more than being the go-to source for great talent.

Look for opportunities to showcase your leadership abilities. Being a good performer is a good start, but your leadership abilities are what drive your potential. You don't have to gain or demonstrate this ability solely in your role or company. Volunteering for a non-profit or participating in an employee resource group are great developmental opportunities. Opportunities are abundant, if you decide to see them as such.

Stop waiting to be picked. Instead of waiting to become a gem, you can make yourself one. To make a crystal, you need the right ingredients (skills, competencies), temperature (environment), pressure (challenge), time (long enough for you to start seeing changes), and space (it is hard to grow in a very confined space).

Get a second, third, or fourth opinion on your appraisal. Not everyone is qualified to assess your value. The value they see in you could depend on several factors. For example, a leader who is looking for someone to stabilize the business may not see value in someone who is a disruptor. Sometimes, we remember the one "bad" thing someone said about us and let that be how we see ourselves, even if others have countered that perspective. If you are consistently getting the same constructive feedback, it may mean you didn't fully comprehend or act on the feedback you got.

SHINE YOUR LIGHT

Hands down, one of my favorite songs growing up was, *This Little Light of Mine*. When I got to the part that said, "I'm going to let it shine," I made sure everyone knew how serious I was by trying to sing as loud as the choir. While growing up in the church, I heard sermons where my pastor quoted Matthew 5:14, "You are the light of the world," and Matthew 5:16, "Let your light so shine before men, that they may see your good works." The verses inform us that we all have light within, and we have a responsibility to use it so others may see the positive things we are doing. The staging process requires you to share what you learn with others because you never know the impact it may have. I want to reemphasize the importance of shining your light in a natural way. Your best self will always be your authentic self–because that is who people want to build a relationship with.

Real World, Real Things Moment:
Drive By

My wife and I enjoy driving through neighborhoods we like at night to check out the homes we've seen for sale. You never know who could drive by your "house" or what time of day they will choose to do so. You never know when an opportunity will arise, so you have to make sure you are always at your best. You want to be the home whose light is always shining brightest on a dark street.

SNIP

Buyers are looking at everything when shopping for homes, and a seller who cuts corners is likely cutting their potential revenue. Shortcuts often shortchange results. This is why I emphasize following a process and remembering the significance of sequence.

Let's say a homeowner focused on curb appeal. If the interior is the complete opposite of the exterior, they may not get a second chance to make a good impression. **Do not make the mistake of being all shine and no substance.**

WHO AM I?

Do you think of curb appeal as relating to your appearance? Being visible? Standing out? Fitting in? Knowing how others see you? If you answered yes to any of the above, you are correct. Let's summarize them under *personal branding.*

Before continuing, I must admit that personal branding has been overused and drifted away from its original intent. These days, the focus of personal branding is on creating an image, managing your social media presence, and developing personal branding statements for resumes and interviews. While personal branding encompasses all of these, there was one thing I was looking for that I did not come across.

IF YOU DO NOT CREATE YOUR OWN PERSONAL BRAND, ONE WILL BE CREATED FOR YOU.

A brand is a person's instinctual reaction to a product, service, or company. Our brains are wired to notice what's different, and our gut confirms it. The foundation of a brand is trust, just like in a relationship. Your personal brand is directly correlated to your relationships with people. People will trust your brand when your experience consistently meets or beats their expectations. Would you rather trust your brain and gut when deciding if someone is trustworthy or take their word for it?

Real World, Real Things Moment:
Control

Having a personal brand created for you is not always a bad thing. When I was in high school, my girlfriend gave me the nickname, "The Total Package." I promise I'm not making that up. Once I embraced it, I owned it. It was something I strived to live up to. Senior year, I was voted "Best All Around." However, not all personal brands follow the same path. We all know people we consider shy, pretentious, and guarded who would vehemently disagree with those descriptions. This is another example of how blind spots can shape people's perceptions. If you do not want to be at the mercy of people's perceptions, control your personal brand and accept the responsibility that comes with deciding to do so.

SUPER NATURAL VS. SUPERNATURAL

For some, proactively managing their brand requires hard work and dedication. It can be daunting playing a character rather than being genuine. Your personal brand should be an honest depiction of your words, actions and habits. They are the foundation of your character. Your character lets people know exactly what to expect during each encounter with you. It also lets them know when you are acting out of character. Your brand should be something natural—it's instinctual. Some people confuse personal branding with just "acting the part." It is okay to look up to someone and want to pattern yourself after them, but you still have to make it your own.

<u>Real World, Real Things Moment:</u>
Crying at Work is a Sign of Authentic Leadership

I recently had a debate with a couple of friends about the best baseball movies of all time. Some of their choices were *Bull Durham*, *Field of Dreams*, *42*, *The Sandlot*, and *Brewster's Millions*. I was the odd man out with *A League of Their Own*. If you have seen the movie, your first thought was probably, "There's no crying in baseball!"

While it was a memorable scene, in my opinion, it was the most inaccurate statement in the movie. For any sports fan reading this, you can probably think of at least five memorable moments when one of the toughest, most dominant athletes in the world cried. I searched the top ten crying moments in sports history. The list included Michael Jordan, Terrell Owens, Brett Favre,

Chris Bosh, Roger Federer, and Mike Schmidt. Does anything stand out about this list?

If it didn't hit you in the face ,pun intended, there was no mention of any female athletes. This made me stop to think about why. It also made me question why crying was accepted in sports but not the workplace.

My search for articles and studies on crying at work revealed the same bias from *A League of Their Own*. Most were about why women shouldn't cry at work. It asserted that women lose their credibility when they show emotions in the workplace. What I find interesting about this is the fact that there is no written rule outright banning crying in the workplace. I think this has been generally accepted is because men are expected to be tough and show little emotion. Since men have historically been leaders in companies, the male experience has often set the cultural norms.

Sylvia Ann Hewlett, founder and CEO of Center for Talent Innovation and author of *Executive Presence: The Missing Link Between Merit and Success* highlighted an issue I have always had with the term executive presence., I feel it is a trait not often associated with female leaders. She states, "Executive presence is signaling to the world that you have what it takes—that you are leadership material. Senior leaders consistently report that crying detracts from one's executive presence, which rests on three pillars: gravitas (how you act), communication (how you speak) and appearance (how you look). Crying, I found in my research, is just one of a menu of communication blunders that, in a mere instant, can suck the executive presence right out of you."

As you read, you may go back and forth with what you agree with, especially since I've only presented one perspective. Remember, context matters. Crying at work is not a black and white scenario. The reason, setting, and frequency all influence its impact on others. We are all humans that spend most of our time at work where we are asked to bring our authentic selves. Crying at appropriate moments can express a vulnerability and authenticity that strengthens executive presence and the connection with colleagues rather than diminishes it. However, if overdone, it can have the opposite effect.

I have had female co-workers cry in front of me. I was humbled and honored that they trusted me enough to show their vulnerability knowing it would have no impact on their credibility. I have also seen male leaders at my company shed tears in very public settings, which inspired me and strengthened my connection to my company. Almost two years ago, I cried for the first time at work as we honored a friend and colleague we lost to cancer. It was the most liberating professional experience because I didn't have to hold back my emotions.

What do you believe is your personal brand?

_____

_____

_____

_____

_____

WHO AM I TO YOU?

If you are struggling to come up with an answer, ask your close friends, co-workers, or family members what your personal brand is. Cast a broad net that covers various social environments to see where there are similarities and differences. Ask them what words they would use to describe you and what having a relationship with you is like. Included in their responses will be things you like and possibly don't like. Be sure to reference the earlier steps discussed about receiving feedback. Sometimes the biggest insight is that people think more highly of you than you do of yourself.

Keep in mind, you may hear very different things from each person you ask. If you do, it's okay. It can be extremely challenging to have your brand be the same with everyone you know or have known. All I ask is that once you discover or create your personal brand, strive to be the same person in every encounter and setting. When you start to see yourself as a brand, your perspective will evolve, and you will become more mindful and intentional about your choices. You will commit to continuously assessing and shaping it as you evolve.

Real World, Real Things Moment:
Etch-A-Sketch

If you don't like your brand, re-brand yourself! You will not be the first or last person to hit the reset button. Consider the following individuals and companies who bounced back from a bad situation or re-branded themselves: Bill Clinton, Robert Downey Jr., Britney Spears, Michael Vick, Mike Tyson, Apple, Starbucks, Target, Wal-Mart, UPS, Old Spice, and Hyundai.

I mentioned earlier my battle with my ego. While I didn't know it was a problem, many people I knew were well aware. I had a brand of arrogance. Once I was aware, I started making different choices about my attitude, beliefs, and behaviors and slowly shifted my brand to one that aligned with who I genuinely wanted to be.

TOOT IT, BUT DON'T BLOW IT!

Managing your brand is not only about self-promotion. It plays a part, but is not the leading role. The staging process was designed to help you uncover and understand your story so that when you share it, you can help others better understand who you are. The people who seem happiest assert it because they get to be their authentic self, day in and day out. When you have done your homework, decluttered, cleaned, made repairs, and worked on your curb appeal, it is then time to inspire others by telling your story.

After reading this chapter and taking some time to reflect, I am now aware of:

_____

_____

_____

_____

The key ideas I wish to remember and share are:

_____

_____

_____

_____

I am going to apply what I have discovered by:

_____

_____

_____

_____

I am going to ask the following individual (s) to hold me accountable:

_____

_____

_____

_____

I will share my progress with them on (insert date):

_____/_____/_____

Things to remember:

- Do not try to dim your light. It is your competitive advantage.
- You never know when opportunity will stop by,

so make sure you've done what's needed so it can find you.

- If you do not create your own brand, one will be created for you.
- Trust is the foundation of a good relationship with yourself and others.
- Your authentic self is your best self.

CHAPTER 7
INSPIRE

SAY WHAT?

We are entering the final stretch of the staging process. Staging involves more than just preparing the interior and exterior of the home. Maybe the most important part is how you tell the home's story. I spoke with several friends and family members who work in real estate about what it takes to write a great listing. They told me the keys are to be honest, be specific, provide motivation, and highlight unseen amenities. One notable comment was, "Omission is not considered an offense."

While most people think it's simple to write a real estate posting, it is actually quite difficult. Many companies specialize in helping agents and homeowners craft listings that give them the best shot at motivating a potential buyer. Notice the significant overlap in what it takes to write a compelling real estate listing and what it takes to effectively tell your story. The last stage of the process underscores the importance of communication. How you tell your story impacts your ability to inspire and influence others.

Effective communication is based on being able to answer a few questions:

- Who is your audience?
- What are you saying?
- Why does it matter?

- How are you saying it?

Below, I matched two elements from a great real estate listing with two elements of good communication.

Real estate: providing motivation
vs.
Good communication: how you are saying it

Providing motivation addresses how you are saying it. Great storytellers speak with passion, as it is both contagious and motivating. I have received solicited and unsolicited feedback that I infuse passion into my talks or presentations. When asked how, my answer is always the same. I just tell the truth. If you believe in what you're saying, it comes across to the audience.

Real estate: highlighting unseen amenities
vs.
Good communication: why does it matter?

Highlighting unseen amenities ties in nicely to why it matters. Starting with *why* focuses you on purpose. Sometimes you have to ask yourself *why* several times to get to a purpose people can really connect with. Since your purpose is shaped by personal experiences only you have, that becomes your competitive advantage. The unseen amenity of any home that cannot be duplicated is the story of the home.

With all forms of communication, it is important to understand that omission is not a sin. That's not to mean you should lie, but there are certain things that are okay to keep to yourself or only share with certain people. My rationale for making this point is twofold. First, you cannot control how someone will react to the information you share. Second, sometimes telling a part of your story involves speaking about someone else in a negative light. At the end of the day, the choice is yours. Just make sure you are prepared to deal with all the possible outcomes of sharing your story, especially to those that haven't earned the right to know you well.

THE CLASSICS

The oral tradition of storytelling moves people emotionally. Stories keep traditions and cultures alive because the emotional connection lasts longer in memory. Great stories are built around captivating events and new discoveries. Written stories have the same effect. The classic books are worth rereading because of the experience. Each time you read them you have a different interpretation and discussing it ignites curiosity. Their influence never fades because they tether themselves to our memories. This is what you should strive for in your story. Everyone that's been with you on your journey should know your story and be able to tell it almost as well as you can. If they can't, it is your responsibility to make sure that they can.

UNDEFEATED OR UNFORGETTABLE?

I'm not exactly sure when I became a fan of boxing, but I'll never forget February 11th, 1990, when I watched in shock as "Iron" Mike Tyson crawled on the canvas unable to find his mouthpiece, legs, or will to continue. The unbeatable had just tasted defeat for the first time. No one expected him to lose that fight or any fight. It is one of the better known fights in boxing. Almost 30 years later, details still emerge about the events leading up to and after the bout. That night underscored the unpredictability of getting in the ring and why every match, no matter the opponent, is a coin toss. While Tyson would never be undefeated again, there was no doubt he would never be forgotten.

Let's play a little game. Review the list of names below and count how many you know from each column. Even if you aren't a boxing fan, you can play along.

Column A	**Column B**
Muhammed Ali	Michael Loewe
Oscar De La Hoya	Sven Ottke
Roberto Duran	Ike Ibeabuchi
Julio Cesar Chavez	Harry Simon
Sugar Ray Leonard	Edwin Valero
George Foreman	Terry Marsh
Joe Louis	Ji-Won Kim

I am going to guess you recognized more names from column A than column B. You may not have even known that the names in column B were boxers. Both columns are all members of the World Boxing Federation Hall of Fame. Those in column A have lost multiple fights while column B is undefeated. For most of the fighters on the left, they returned stronger after each defeat. They became better boxers after each loss. Their weaknesses were exposed, and they learned from them. However, you know them all because they were storytellers. They had unmistakable brands. Their triumphs and defeats are legendary because audiences had an emotional connection with them.

There is a lot to learn about taking risks from boxing. Having an undefeated record could mean you haven't taken enough risks. Getting in the ring, even when you think you are outclassed, could completely change your life. We have become so obsessed with winning that we overlook the opportunity discovered in defeat. One loss doesn't prevent you from ever experiencing victory. In fact, stories about overcoming defeat tend to be the most memorable.

On a related note, one of the last directions fighters receive from the referee is to protect themselves at all times. For a defensive fighter, this comes naturally. For an offensive fighter, this may leave them exposed, much like blind spots. Examples of protecting yourself from those "blind spots" may include developing diverse relationships, regularly seeking feedback from various groups, and acquiring additional skills that will make you more balanced.

Numbers in parentheses reflect number of losses:
Joe Louis (3), Muhammed Ali (5), George Foreman (5), Roberto Duran (16), Sugar Ray Leonard (3), Oscar De La Hoya (6), and Julio Cesar Chavez (6)

Real World, Real Things Moment:
A Closed Mouth Doesn't Get Fed

I had been at my company for a few years and was starting to make a name for myself within my department but wasn't on the radar of senior management. I kept my head down and worked hard but wasn't afraid to volunteer for more work, especially if I believed it would be mutually beneficial.

One of my mentors from another company suggested I ask my peers which leader they admired the most and why. Following his direction, I noticed one name kept coming up. Then, he suggested to meet with that leader. When the day came, I walked into her office, formally introduced myself, and told her I only had two questions. First, what was going to be her legacy? She didn't flinch. It was if she has already thought about it her whole career. Her answer reflected what I expected based on what I had learned about her brand and character. My second question was how could I become part of her legacy? She paused, tilted her head to the left, pushed back from her desk, locked her fingers, and responded with her trademark, "Okay!" It was the kind of *okay* that showed she admired my audacity and was curious to see if I was worthy. She told me about a role she just created for a group she was asked to lead and offered it to me on the spot. I accepted.

After succeeding in that role, she gave me a leadership opportunity. While in that role, she sponsored me to attend a premier leadership development program that had such a profound impact on me, it became the catalyst for my first book. It is important to note that I never officially worked for my sponsor. The roles I took on were voluntary. But, she made it clear to my management the impact I had, and her sponsorship put me on the radar of other leaders in the organization. To this day, she is someone I connect with regularly for personal and professional advice and I am so grateful that someone once told me a closed mouth doesn't get fed, even though I had no idea what it meant at the time. Having the courage to ask to be part of her legacy is a tipping point in my story. She actually wrote the forward to my first book. This is how she told our story.

FLASHBACK

When I first began my career in the pharmaceutical industry more than twenty-five years ago, I could have used a book like STAGED! There were several on the market that taught me how to dress, speak, and "go along to get along." But I needed more. At a time when there were few role models I could identify with, I read every book I could find. Still, books that encouraged me to own my career development, clarify my goals, establish a personal brand and celebrate my authentic self were still missing.

*Despite having very few role models, I did successfully climb the corporate ladder. I now have a seat at multiple decision-making tables, both at work and in the global community. While the **journey** was not always simple or what I expected, it was a little easier with a network of individuals who supported, encouraged, and generally "had my back" along the way. They helped me effectively tackle issues everyone faces in the workplace, like getting promoted faster and making a bigger impact. They also provided much needed* *perspective so I did not lose sight of the important things in life.*

STAGED! will take you on a similar journey of self-discovery by giving you the tools to uncover your strengths, understand your opportunities, establish your personal brand, and embrace your story.

I have known Conrod Kelly for many years, first as an MBA recruit (the one that got away!) and later as a rising talent at Merck & Co., Inc. (we got him back!). He is a lifelong learner, constantly building his knowledge base. He is a highly creative thinker who consistently seeks new ways to add value. He is a teacher who provides compelling lessons on how to gain a competitive edge in a tough business environment. But most of all, he is a leader who always inspires others to do their best work. I am grateful our paths have crossed.

I urge you to read STAGED! with pen in hand. Take time to honor the process and reflect on the questions; be thoughtful about your responses. What will emerge is a plan to help you become your best self. Once you have been "Staged," you will have the knowledge you need to take control of your career and build a life where you are the "writer, producer and lead actor."

STAGED! allows you to explore, reflect and - most importantly - dream big.

The power to transform your career and your life is closer than you think. STAGED! will show you how!

Charlotte O. McKines
Vice President, Global Marketing
Merck & Co., Inc.

SPONSORED BY

Charlotte spoke about the role her sponsors played in her career by encouraging and supporting her while helping her tackle issues and gain perspective. As one of my sponsors, she has connected me with individuals, open doors for me, and even built doors when they didn't exist. Sponsors are important because in most situations you won't be in the room to tell your own story.

You may be wondering if you have a sponsor. Most of the time, you know who they are. Sometimes, you don't. I have formed positive opinions of people who I don't intimately know from someone I trust and respect that does know them. Remember, someone is always watching.

Even then, you may have to groom someone to be your sponsor. Keep an eye out for people you believe can help you achieve your goals. Be prepared to let them know what you bring to the table. This increases their confidence that an investment in you is a sure bet. The absolute best advice I have for finding a sponsor is first becoming one.

Real World, Real Things Moment:
The Best Gifts Make You and Others Better

Toward the end of last year, I participated in an all-day workshop with a large, diverse group of attendees. Typical of these types of workshops, the session started with an icebreaker. The question was what our favorite Christmas gift growing up was. Christmas was more about practical gifts in my family --- clothes, socks, pajamas, and underwear—so I struggled to come up with one gift that was truly memorable. As others gave passionate stories, I got frustrated because I couldn't come up with something. Eventually, I remembered a gift, but not who it was from.

The question kept bothering me until I finally figured out why. Gary Chapman, author of *The Five Love Languages*, says there are five ways that people give or receive love in any relationship: words of affirmation, acts of service, receiving gifts, quality time, and physical touch. The dominant love languages in my family have always been words of affirmation and acts of service. Through the lens of love languages, if I were asked again about my best gift, the answer would be someone believing in me through their words and actions.

The best example of someone believing in me is the day my mother quit her job so she could watch me give a five-minute speech. That gift inspired me to believe in myself as much as she did. Self-belief plays a significant role in personal and professional growth. Ralph Waldo Emerson said, "Our chief want is someone who will inspire us to be what we could be." Can you think of anyone that can benefit from you believing in them? Becoming their sponsor? Telling their story?

Every day, we wake up with the incredible power to change someone's life with a few words, a kind gesture, or our undivided attention. While we are currently obsessed with speculating how high the Dow will go, there is no greater return than the investment we make in others because in doing so, it helps us grow and shape our legacy.

Matthew McConaughey's Oscar acceptance speech had a profound impact on me. He said each day, he needs something to look up to, something to look forward to, and something to chase. I offer this adaptation to Mr. McConaughey's words: each day, believe in something greater than you, believe in yourself, and believe in someone else.

COMING FROM WHERE I AM FROM

The journey to becoming the best and real you, starts with understanding and appreciating the story of your life. Autobiographies tend to include common themes of overcoming difficulties, failures, or tragedies. Your story may stem from similar experiences or rich, positive ones. Positive or negative, those experiences should be used to bring meaning to your life. Your story provides the context for your experiences and through it, you can find the voice you need to inspire yourself and others.

Telling your story is an opportunity to take people on a journey that lets them connect with you in a deeper way or inspire them to embark on one of their own. Your story is a powerful engine, something no one can duplicate or take away from you. Having a strong intrinsic, motivator is a competitive advantage. See it as an eternal flame that can withstand any storm that may enter your life.

Real World, Real Things Moment:

Words Matter

I recently went on vacation with my wife, Joy. On the way to the airport, we ran into traffic that delayed us an hour. While sitting in traffic, I said under my breath, "Everything happens for a reason," before drifting off to sleep. After arriving at the airport, we had difficulty checking in. We stood at the counter for about thirty minutes as the agent tried to resolve the issue. A minute later, I said to my wife, "If there is a will, there is a way," and continued to wait patiently. About an hour after we arrived, the tickets were issued and we made our flight. Shortly after takeoff, I started reading the Wall Street Journal and I came across the article, "One Habit to Make You Happier Today." What caught my attention more than the title was the subhead that read, "Repeating a positive phrase, or mantra, to yourself creates new pathways between neurons in your brain, conditioning you to feel calmer and healthier." Without knowing it, I had been using various personal mantras to get me through the hiccups in our travel. My wife even commented on how calm I had been throughout the ordeal.

Those mantras I repeated came from my mother. They were the rules for how she lived her life and parented me and my siblings. Most personal mantras are tied into a belief system and are often inherited. They are a major part of our upbringing. The first time I heard the word *mantra* was in my strategic marketing class in business school. One of my professors talked about brand mantras being short, three-to-five-word phrases that capture the essence of a brand. A brand mantra is not typically a tagline or slogan or something you would use publicly. Nike's tagline is "Just Do It" but its brand mantra is "Authentic Athletic Performance." Brand mantras help brands be focused and consistent and ensure the trust of customers and employees.

My friend Sonia Thompson, an author and INC.com and Forbes contributor, recently wrote. "...science says there is one thing you can do that will significantly improve the performance of a [team]: Believe in them." One way to demonstrate your belief in a team is to have a team mantra. On one of my teams, our mantra was "Epic is Our Standard" and for another team it was "Yes, ICON." These mantras are part of our story. I want to encourage you to develop professional, personal, or even familial mantras that epitomize your story.

HIS STORY

I started *RESTAGED* with the concept of inception because my story boils down to an idea: a couple, along with their four children, immigrate to the United States from Jamaica for a chance at a better life. They put an idea in the mind of their youngest that he was destined to be someone great. He grew to accept that idea and made it his own. The universe responded by putting people, opportunities, obstacles, and adversity in his life to teach him about honesty, humility, determination, and faith.

David, a childhood friend I had to let go of to follow this approach, introduced me to the concept of "What does it cost you to ask?" If I hadn't learned that lesson young, I don't know who or where I would be. That fearlessness supported by my understanding of faith made me grasp the concept that all my asks should be directed above. It is also in His word that I should have no fear. I still have the Bible my mother gave me when I went off to FAMU with verses she left on my answering machine or texted scribbled on blank pages. Below are a few worth looking up:

- Joshua 1:9
- Psalm 27:1, 34:4, 56:3-4, 118:6
- Isaiah 41:10,13
- 1 Peter 3:13-14

My mother introduced me to the mantra "What God has for you, it is for you." Through it, I learned patience and acceptance.

At this point, you must be thinking I've lived a charmed life. I promise I have not. I've had to deal with things I wouldn't wish on my worst enemy. But sharing those stories with you would not help me accomplish my goal for you. It would also require me to speak about others in a way that doesn't help them. The last reason is because I live by the home staging mental model, which means a lot of those memories have been through the decluttering, cleaning, and repair process, and may no longer support my current goals.

ONCE UPON A TIME

As we draw closer to the end, we end up where we started. Telling your story boils down to purpose, process, preparation, practice, and persistence. Great storytellers obsessively prepare. Their story is always a work in progress. They learn how to tell the short version, the long version, and the audience-dependent version. They practice so much that they can improvise on the drop of a dime. You too can be a great storyteller by knowing your story inside and out. It should be easy because it's yours! You have lived it your whole life. It is your identity and purpose. The process you have gone through reading this book will make for a great story.

In doing your homework, you should have found new insights. The investment you made to declutter your memory of things that can't help you grow, clean up things so they don't creep back into your narrative, and repair relationships that are a foundation to your development, has healed you on the inside. This enables your authentic self to shine and invites others in or permits them to voluntarily wander into your life. Now your story is ready to inspire them. The stage is set.

You did it! You've been STAGED!

After reading this chapter and taking time to reflect, I am now aware of:

_____

_____

_____

_____

The key ideas I wish to remember and share are:

_____

_____

_____

_____

I am going to apply what I have discovered by:

_____

_____

_____

_____

I am going to ask the following individual(s) to hold me accountable:

_____

_____

_____

_____

I will share my progress with them on:

_____/_____/_____

Things to remember:

- Your story is your competitive advantage. No one else has experienced your life but you.

- Make sure you are not the only one who knows or can tell your story.

- Your story is the seed that is rooted in your purpose.

ACKNOWLEDGMENTS

I would first like to thank God for everything!

Thank you to my wife, friend, and life partner Joy, who continues to support me on this journey we call life. In addition to her unconditional love, she gave me the best gift in the world, my daughter Nola Grace.

Nola, thank you for teaching me patience, perspective, and the importance of boundaries.

Thank you to my parents, siblings, and family for your love and support.

Thank you to my hand-selected family, my friends, who continue to support and inspire me. You give me a safe space to be 200% me.

Thank you to everyone I've ever encountered who told me the truth, whether I wanted to hear it or not.

I want to thank Ms. Zanetta Lynn Newbern for reinforcing the power of humility. Although you are no longer physically here with us, you gave me something that will stay with me until we meet again.

I SPEAK YOUR NAMES

My story is built on the fact that along the way, someone always believed in me. I've always carried that belief like a debt I must repay. As the saying goes, to whom much is given, much is expected.

The following seven women, the number of perfection, had a profound impact on my life because of their words, vision, actions, love, and support.

Mrs. Juanita Albury—For recognizing my gift.

Ms. Thelma White Horton—For making me mentally tough.

Mrs. Kathleen Hoffman—For making me respect my role as a leader

Mom – For introducing me to the power of faith

Mrs. Josephine Stinson—For trusting your gut.

Dr. Sybil Mobley—For having the vision to create a program that accepted nothing less than excellence.

Ms. Jane Quinn—For giving me additional time to learn. Who knew that all I had to do was ask for it?

Mrs. Albury

My kindergarten teacher, Mrs. Albury, saw right through the quiet boy from Jamaica who had a funny accent. She told me she felt it in her spirit that there was something special about me. She noticed I was pretty advanced, so she gave me additional, more complex, assignments. She even had me spend the weekend at her house putting together puzzles and playing word games. When she had seen enough, she encouraged my mother to get me tested for the gifted program. She took us to the testing center herself. Her investment in me afforded me a private school education within the Dade County public school system, which gave me advantages I would not have had if she had not pushed me.

Ms. Horton

Ms. Horton was my fourth-grade teacher. She challenged me to be mentally tough. She gave me assignments she knew I couldn't complete to see how I responded to adversity. She wanted to see how long I would work before giving up. What I initially thought were lessons in adversity were actually exercises in humility. She was the first teacher to get me to say, "I don't know." Another of her tricks was to switch me from the winning team to the losing team in the middle of a class competition to see if I was still willing to fight as the underdog. Her experiment taught me to see the opportunity in setbacks. What I learned from being up was just as valuable, if not more so, when I was down. Maybe the most confusing and influential of her antics was calling our entire class names, like nerds or geeks, to desensitize us. She taught us not to shy away from our gifts or talents but to embrace them.

Mrs. Hoffman

Mrs. Hoffman was my teacher from sixth through eighth grade and was one of the toughest by far. She pushed me to embrace my role as a leader and respect it. She held me accountable for my actions because of the influence I had over my peers. Her husband was the assistant principal and I spent a lot of time in his office or detention because of my behavior. She was the first to point out to me how my behavior could undermine my achievements if not checked.

My Mother

In the 7th grade, a life-altering thing happened. I was chosen as Peer Mediator of the Year for the state of Florida and was selected to give a speech at the Peer Mediator Conference. My mother's boss changed his mind about giving her the day off the day before the conference. In what I would call the most courageous act of faith, she quit her job so she could watch me speak. It is a moment I've never forgotten, and it introduced me to faith. On the drive home, she told me our steps had already been ordered and everything was happening according to God's will. Could she have known that moment would change my life forever?

Mrs. Stinson

In the summer of my tenth-grade year, I encountered Josephine Stinson, the lead teacher for the Business and Finance Academy at the brand-new magnet school Coral Reef Senior High School. Because it was new, in spirit of fairness, students were selected by raffle. Unfortunately, my name was not selected for the magnet I wanted. A few weeks later, I got a call from Mrs. Stinson telling me she had one spot left in her academy and selected me from a list of hundreds because my name sounded like someone who was going to be famous.

Mrs. Stinson and I developed a good relationship. We used to arrive at school about the same time (I was dropped off at least an hour before school started) and I helped make coffee and set up the room for her corporate advisory board. She let me to sit in on the meetings, which was priceless.

Early in my senior year, Florida A & M University was having a scholarship banquet and asked my principal to send four students. I was one of 435 seniors, but Mrs. Stinson insisted I be selected as one of the four to attend the banquet. On the day of the banquet, everything that could go wrong did. Our ride was late, it rained, and we got lost. My mother prayed so hard, nearly crushing my hands. We got there just before the event was over and I was immediately handed a paper to write down my GPA and SAT score. Ten minutes later, I was standing up front with the president of the university holding a full scholarship.

The service I provided to my school and lead teacher, in addition to my preparation that resulted in high GPA and SAT scores, provided me a full ride for my Bachelors and Masters degrees. On that day, I walked away knowing the multiplier effect that service provides. My upbringing was rooted in the idea of hard work and service. I learned to lead by learning to serve. I received because I gave. I realized at a very early age that my purpose was service. When I am engaged in service, my energy is unlimited.

Dr. Sybil Mobley
Three months after turning eighteen, I entered the Five-year MBA program at Florida A & M University's School of Business and Industry (SBI). From my first on campus until graduation, I had the opportunity to interact with countless CEOs, Presidents, and executives from Fortune 500 companies. I also served as the CEO of one of the nineteen student-run companies that supported our school.

Dean Mobley referred to us as her SBI Superstars because she was preparing us to compete with the best and brightest because we would be the most prepared and well-rounded. My experience in SBI demonstrated the power high expectations, positive reinforcement, and exposure could have on students.

Ms. Jane Quinn.

Working for Jane Quinn was a masterclass in leadership. She led the Pediatric Vaccines business at GlaxoSmithKline (GSK) during my residency. Because of the structure of the five-year MBA program, our internships would be our only work experience prior to graduation. During the graduate portion, we could do residency programs of six to twelve months as a full-time employee. My residency with GSK was approved for 8-months. I was working on a small team that was responsible for launching a new adolescent vaccine. Jane led an all-male team with style and grace. She was wicked smart but didn't use it to intimidate you. She exuded confidence and executive presence but wasn't afraid to let her hair down. I'm sure she eventually figured it out, but I synchronized my schedule with hers. We would be the only ones on the floor in the morning and would have in-depth conversations about the business and life. We would also be the last ones on the floor some nights and would bounce ideas off each other. As my time was nearing the end, she asked me if I wanted to stay on to finish launching the drug I had been working on. I checked with my business school and they gave the green light. One of my other classmates who was with me at GSK did the same and I think we still hold the record for the longest residency with sixteen months. Her willingness to have me stay on is what made me so competitive upon graduation. I was going up against students who did a summer internship between their first and second year of graduate school while I had three years of pharmaceutical brand marketing, product launch experience, and endless hours of knowledge and insights that Jane shared with me over the sixteen months.

I came across this letter recently that I sent to my family as most thought the extension of my residency meant I was dropping out of school.

Date: September 22, 2004
Subject: Reasons Why Conrod Sebastian Jason Kelly is Staying in Philadelphia

I am pursuing a Master of Business Administration. The majority of individuals pursuing the same degree are a minimum of 27 years old with 5 years' worth of work experience. As I am preparing to enter the job market, it is important for you to understand the advantage these individuals will have over me if I do not have more work experience:

1. They are older than I am and seen as more mature
2. They have more real-world work experience where my experience could be viewed as just internship experience
3. They can provide results of their work, where if I leave now, all I can say is that I planned the work

Staying at GSK for a year and a half as Associate Product Manager on a launch brand, I will be able to gain valuable work experience and knowledge about my industry and career of choice. This opportunity will erase the perceived maturity gap because of my age and will amplify my accomplishments as prospective employers will see that each year I have grown based on my increased responsibilities, complexity of my projects, and accomplishments. This experience could be what lands me a six-figure salary upon graduation. My goal is not to have a job but a career, and I feel this decision helps me do so. Not only will I be an attractive candidate to this company, but also to several other companies who have started recruiting me to come and work for their organizations.

I am sure that you all have come to the conclusion that I want to stay in Philadelphia because I am making money. Well, let's take a closer look at this money thing. I am paying off a car that I hope to own by the time I leave here. I will have enough money put away to pay for my expenses once I go back to school. Additionally, after learning a lot about credit, investing, and how to save, not having student loans and credit card debt will give me a head start to financial independence. Therefore, it is critical I stay here to get more work experience, pay off all my bills, increase my credit score, and save money. This is how God revealed it to me.

Finally, being in a place I don't know has helped me grow in many ways. My level of independence has increased significantly. You would be surprised how spending time alone helps you see yourself in a whole different light. I have seen the good and the bad, and am working on improving both. I am meeting people, seeing new places, becoming more cultured through my tastes for music, arts, food, literature, etc. Will I finish school? I can't believe you all are even thinking like that. Did you have to tell me I was going to college? I knew I was going for a long time and I knew I was going to make a way for myself to go. I have seven classes left. These internships count towards graduation and I am taking a class now while I am here, and I will probably take another before I leave. I am no quitter, especially when it comes to my own goals. I told you both this the minute I graduated from high school. What I do now is for the benefit of my dreams and goals. It just happens that we share the same dreams and goals so we will both be happy. I hope you don't misunderstand my tone, but I wanted to make sure I was clear. If you have any questions, please feel free to contact me.

Love always,
Jason

MY ADVANTAGE

I am my competitive advantage.
My faith is my competitive advantage.

My fearlessness is my competitive advantage.
My persistence is my competitive advantage.
My preparation is my competitive advantage.

My passion is my competitive advantage.
My purpose is my competitive advantage.
My service is my competitive advantage.

My journey is my competitive advantage.
My voice is my competitive advantage
My story is my competitive advantage.

Our deepest fear is not that we are inadequate. Our deepest fear is that we are powerful beyond measure. It is our light, not our darkness, that most frightens us. We ask ourselves, who am I to be brilliant, gorgeous, talented, fabulous? Actually, who are you not to be? You are a child of God. Your playing small doesn't serve the world. There is nothing enlightened about shrinking so that other people won't feel insecure around you. We are all meant to shine, as children do. We were born to make manifest the glory of God that is within us. It's not just in some of us; it's in everyone. And as we let our own light shine, we unconsciously give others permission to do the same. As we're liberated from our own fear, our presence automatically liberates others.

—Marianne Williamson

ABOUT THE AUTHOR

Conrod S. J. Kelly founded STAGES, a career development company, to help individuals on a larger scale after years of one-on-one career coaching. His first book, *STAGED!* introduced the staging philosophy and process. In *RESTAGED*, Conrod leverages the process to get input on his first book and has written a new version based on that feedback. He draws on years of experience at companies such as Johnson & Johnson, GlaxoSmithKline, and Merck, along with his many years as a student of personal and professional development, to motivate and inspire others.

He is originally from Kingston, Jamaica, and grew up in South Florida. Conrod and his wife, Joy, reside in the Greater Philadelphia area with their daughter, Nola Grace.

APPENDIX OF SELECT WRITING FROM CONROD S.J. KELLY ON ADVERSITY

I. The Secret to a Comeback is Halftime, August 17, 2017

1st Half

Just about all the major sports are played in halves. You've probably heard the phrase, "Everyone loves a good comeback." That is especially true in sports, where halftime is usually the turning point. I'm always curious to know which words were spoken, who spoke them, and what adjustments were made in those fifteen minutes to produce the greatest comeback games.

In Super Bowl LI, the New England Patriots set a record by overcoming a 28 to 3 deficit to beat the Atlanta Falcons. During the post victory news conference, every reporter wanted to know what was said during halftime to spark the turnaround. According to wide receiver Julian Edelman, the coaches said, "Let's just play one play at a time. We can't worry about things we can't control. Let's just worry about what we can control." More striking than the absence of a big, emotional speech was that most players said they stayed calm and reflected on the head coach's mantra of "Do your job."

Halftime

As part of my writing routine, once I feel like I've taken a good run at a post, I'll reach out to a few friends to get feedback. Call it my halftime. My friend and INC.com contributor Sonia Thompson gave me the following advice: "I like where this is going. I'd suggest focusing it on the importance of taking a half-time or a 'pause' to regroup. Don't be afraid to weave in personal stories of things that you've done."

2nd Half

Reflecting on how the Patriots overcame adversity led me to two conclusions:

- **Creating a "halftime" provides you with an opportunity to reflect, regroup, and make adjustments**

A mid-year review could be considered a halftime. It allows you to gain feedback, reflect, and make the necessary adjustments to have a strong second half of the year. You can build halftimes into just about any scenario. My personal favorite halftime is my lunch break. After eating my meal, I like to go outside and listen to music or read an article to relax and then focus on how I'm going to finish the second half of the day.

- **The way you react to adversity impacts how you overcome it**

One of my personal mantras is "In every setback, there is a learning opportunity and potential for growth." I've had a tough first half of the year on both a personal and professional level. One of my approaches for getting through tough times is to find moments to be silent and listen for the lesson the adversity is trying to teach me. In doing so, I find encouragement in everything, from articles to books to movies to music. This time however, my biggest source of inspiration has come from connecting with peers and leaders in my company in ways I never would have imagined. Their personal stories and "halftime speeches" have prepared me for my second half comeback.

II. Put Some Pep in Your Pause, Sept 18, 2017

In my last post, "The Secret to a Comeback is Halftime," I spoke about the role of halftimes in comeback victories, specifically highlighting New England's comeback in Super Bowl LI. While most believe big, emotional speeches like the one's seen in Hollywood blockbusters are responsible for turnaround victories, even though they are very entertaining, the Patriot's victory revealed two different reasons:

- Halftimes provide an opportunity to recover, reflect, and make adjustments. No team has proven to be better at making adjustments than New England.
- The way you react to adversity impacts how you overcome it. According to wide receiver Julian Edelman, the coaches said, "Let's just worry about what we can control."

A few days after the post went up, I received a message from Ashley Ridgeway-Washington, the System Director of Human Resources at CHRISTUS Health, with an interesting twist on my perspective. After a few messages back and forth, I asked her if she would be willing to be interviewed for this post. Luckily, she accepted.

Conrod: So, as an HR leader, do you encourage leaders to take halftime breaks?

Ashley: First things first, you forgot to mention concession stand runs and restroom breaks as reasons for halftimes! Now, back to your question. The workplace is not necessarily known for halftime breaks or even "time-outs." In the surgical field, the use of a "time-out" before starting the procedure to ensure the right patient is having the right procedure at the right site has had a significant impact on patient safety. The business world hasn't quite caught on to the notion of the "deliberate pause." At least, not yet.

Conrod: While there may not be a "deliberate" pause, is it fair to assume that they do take pauses?

Ashely: In my experience, leaders do take pauses to issue rallying cries to their teams or the broader organization. Unfortunately, that means most perceive the value of a pause to be greatest when there is adversity and not necessarily as an approach to avoid adversity.

Conrod: So, you are saying that the value of a pause comes before there is adversity?

Ashley: Henry Ford is quoted saying, "Failure is the opportunity to begin again more intellectually." While I understand Mr. Ford's perspective, I believe that great leaders do not wait until failure is imminent to reflect, reinforce, and reenergize—presumably, more intellectually after experiencing learning opportunities from the ongoing journey.

Conrod: Do you think this approach would be viewed positively in an organization? I would suspect some may say it could leave you vulnerable by taking your foot off the gas.

Ashley: Today's leaders manage teams that handle complex problems. While organizations place tremendous focus on developing a strategy and taking action quickly, great leaders guide teams in the process of reflection to improve future outcomes, reinforce trust, and drive accountability. Great leaders also celebrate incremental successes while keeping teams focused on the work that is to be done to move forward successfully.

Conrod: Earlier, you mentioned that pauses can help to reenergize teams. Are you saying that even when a team is doing well, they still need to be reenergized?

Ashley: Of course! By pausing to celebrate wins, recognize individual contributions, map progress, and speak words of encouragement, leaders can breathe life into exhausted teams.

After speaking with Mrs. Ridgeway-Washington, she reminded me that the other team in the locker room at halftime needed the pause just as much as the team facing adversity to ensure they didn't let victory slip through their hands. Our conversation also led me to expand my perspective on "halftimes, timeouts, and pauses," as well as reposition my view of the big emotional speech by thinking about it as more of a pep talk. She helped me realize pep talks can generate a strong performance out of the gate as well as sustain the performance. However, we both agreed that while this is an important skill for a business leader, very few have any training in how to do it or do it well.

According to Daniel McGinn's article, "The Science of Pep Talks," the magic formula for a great pep talk is a combination of direction giving, expressions of empathy, and meaning making.

- Direction giving is defined as providing information about precisely how to do the task at hand.
- Expressions of empathy could include praise, encouragement, gratitude, and acknowledgement of a task's difficulty.
- Meaning making is explaining why, normally through stories, the work impacts customer or community.

If you are or want to be a leader, the time to start exploring the various benefits of pausing and perfecting the art of the pep talk is now.